JAPAN

Maps Matthew & Taylor Associates pages 46 and 47

Contents page Boys taking part in the *Tsuina* festival at the end of winter. The traditions of the festival date back 1,000 years.

Photographic sources Key to positions of illustrations: (T) top, (C) center, (B) bottom, (L) left, (R) right.

Barnaby's Picture Library: 25BL, 29TR, 40TR. BBC Hulton Picture Library: 16T. British Museum: 35TL. Robert Harding Picture Library: 11TL, 22BR, 26TR, 30TC & BR, 31TL, 36–37. S & S Hoare: 18BR, 19TR & CR, 21BL, 28CR, 29TL. International Society for Educational Information: 38BL. Japan Information Center, Counselate General of Japan, New York: 17B. Japan National Tourist Organization: 17T. Japanese Embassy: 15BL, 22BR, 34BR, 36BL, 39TL. Japanese Tourist Office: 14T, 26BL, 36CR. Karen Kasmauski/Woodfin Camp: 32T. Macdonald Library: 31TR & BR/Hugh Oliff: 25TR. Mansell Collection: 9BL. J. March-Penney: 8, 21BR. Hiroyuki Matsumoto/Black Star: 18BL. Pictor: 5–6, 9BR, 20TR, 26–27, 27TR, 28BL, 29BR, 33TR, 35BL, 37BR, 38CR. Recontre: 12BL, 12–13, 13TL & TR, 35TR. Rex Features: 11BL, 17BL, 24TR, 25TL, 27C & BR, 28–29, 29BC, 40BR, 41BL. Royal Navy: 16BR. SEF: Endpapers, 23TL, 27TL, 39BL. E. Shimauchi: 32–33 Francis Skinner: 11TR, 20BR, 21TL, 24BR, 34TR, 35BR. Spectrum Colour Library: 30TR, 37TL & TR, 40C. Richard Tames: 10. Elizabeth Thurley: 41T. Toyota: 19B, 23BL. US Air Force: 17CL. Reverend van Straelen: 28TR. ZEFA: 9T, 11BR, 17R, 41BR.

First published in Great Britain in 1975 by Macdonald Education Ltd.

Adapted and published in the United States in 1987 by Silver Burdett Press, Morristown, N.J.

Revised 1991 by Silver Burdett Press, Englewood Cliffs, N.J.

Library of Congress Cataloging-in-Publication Data

Tames, Richard.
Japan / Richard Tames. — 2nd rev. ed.
p. cm. — (Silver Burdett countries)
Rev. ed. of: Japan, the land and its people.
Rev. ed. 1987. © 1986.
Includes bibliographic references and index.
Summary: Text and photographs introduce life in a country well known for valuing calmness and harmony.
1. Japan—Juvenile literature. [1. Japan.]
I. Tames, Richard. Japan, the land and its people. II. Title. III. Series.
DS806.T292 1991   91-17520
952—dc20   CIP
ISBN 0-382-24246-7 (LSB)   AC

Cover photo: Dave Bartruff

SECOND REVISED EDITION

SILVER BURDETT COUNTRIES

JAPAN

Richard Tames

SILVER BURDETT PRESS

Contents

Land of contrasts

Four-fifths of Japan is mountainous, yet it contains some of the world's largest cities. Two-thirds of its people live packed into only 3% of its land area: space is at a premium, and yet Japanese agriculture can still supply three-quarters of the nation's food. Japanese cities bristle with skyscrapers and the countryside is crossed by highways and high-speed railways; but the land is still vulnerable to typhoons, volcanoes, and earthquakes. The climate, too, displays dramatic contrasts. Northern provinces can be snowbound for months, while to the south, islands in the Ryukyu chain enjoy subtropical conditions.

Energy and harmony

Throughout their long history the Japanese have displayed the characteristics of energy and determination. Villages and cities destroyed by fire or natural disaster have been rebuilt again and again. Defeated in war, the Japanese of today have rebuilt their country quite literally from the ashes. Yet few peoples place more value on calmness and harmony or find more ways to pursue or express these ideals through nature, art, or physical pursuits and skills.

Contrasts not conflicts

Visitors to Japan a century ago were amazed to see ancient traditions and modern technology existing side by side. The contrast is just as striking today. Japan is renowned for its advanced robots but the *kabuki* theater still flourishes. Videos record *samurai* dramas. And a salesclerk is as likely to use an abacus *(soroban)* as an electronic calculator. The perceptions and comments of Western visitors often imply that there must be a conflict between the old and the new, between what has been developed in Japan and what has been adapted from other countries. But perhaps it is the Japanese genius for blending old and new, native and foreign, that best explains the character of the country. Japan seems to be ever changing, and yet essentially the same.

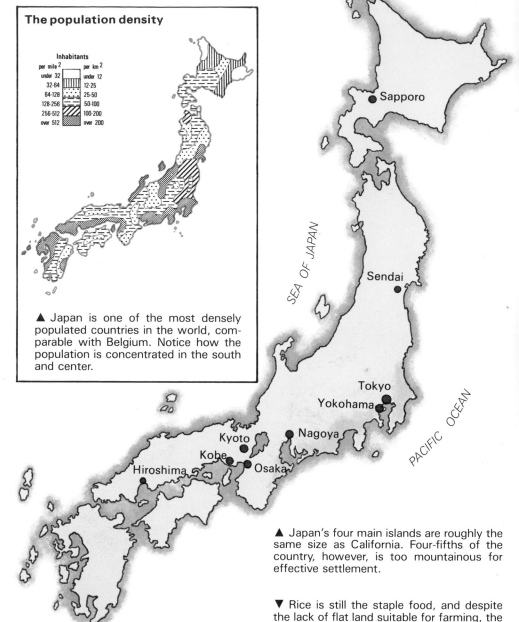

The population density

Inhabitants

per mile²	per km²
under 32	under 12
32-64	12-25
64-128	25-50
128-256	50-100
256-512	100-200
over 512	over 200

▲ Japan is one of the most densely populated countries in the world, comparable with Belgium. Notice how the population is concentrated in the south and center.

▲ Japan's four main islands are roughly the same size as California. Four-fifths of the country, however, is too mountainous for effective settlement.

▼ Rice is still the staple food, and despite the lack of flat land suitable for farming, the country is self-sufficient in this crop.

▲ The bullet train service, inaugurated in 1964 at the time of the Tokyo Olympics, now links the major cities of Honshu and Kyushu. Its speed and efficiency have become famous worldwide, and stand as an effective symbol of Japan's modern technology.

► Japan's long rocky coastline serves as a reminder of the importance of the sea in Japanese history. Fish is still the main source of protein in the Japanese diet, and shipbuilding remains an important industry.

▼ Japan is prone to earthquakes, and in 1923 disaster struck large parts of Tokyo and neighboring Yokohama. Buildings collapsed and caught fire, and about 140,000 people died. Bombing raids in 1945 were even more destructive, but the city was rapidly reconstructed.

The people and their language

All societies consist of individuals who are also members of groups. What makes Japan distinctive is the fact that individual Japanese are so strongly aware that they *are* members of different groups, from the family to the work-team to the nation. The strong sense of group belonging in Japan is expressed through ideals of behavior. There is a proverb that says "The nail that sticks up gets hammered in": the sense of this is "fit in with other people." Conformity to social conventions is expected. Even small children are told "Don't do that, people will laugh at you." Loyalty to superiors — parents, teachers, bosses — is expected because they stand for the authority of the group as a whole.

Language and law

The Japanese language itself expresses the people's keen awareness of others. It has a complicated system of "honorifics," which controls not only how politely one person addresses another but also how they refer to themselves. One result of the strong Japanese awareness of others is that the law is used less often than in western countries to settle disputes. There are western-style laws and lawyers but generally speaking, in business, just as in everyday life, Japanese prefer to trust to good human relations rather than written contracts. The force of convention means that sometimes Japan strikes outsiders as a country in which everyone knows everyone else's business. This may be true; but one good effect of this is a very low crime rate because detection is much more certain than in western countries.

Calmness and laughter

Japanese are often referred to by foreigners as "inscrutable." This may reflect the fact that being isolated by history and geography, the Japanese have been rather wary when dealing with *gaikokujin* (foreigners — literally, "outside country persons"). It also reflects the fact that Japanese admire people who can keep their emotions under control. But they do like to laugh — if everyone else does.

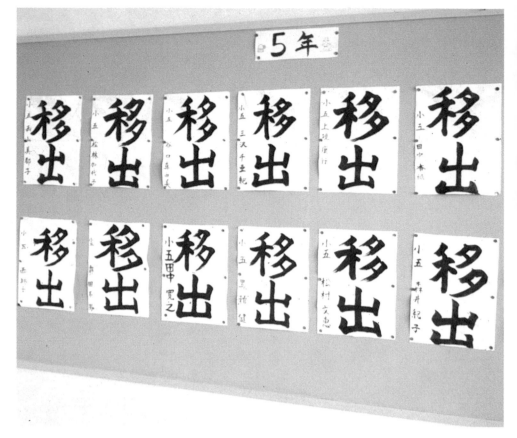

▲ The difficult Japanese system of writing combines Chinese characters (known as *kanji*) and two phonetic "syllabaries" (known as *hiragana* and *katakana*). A syllabary is a set of symbols, each of which represents one syllable. They can be written in a variety of styles, according to whether one is writing a poem or a poster. The art of the calligrapher is highly respected.

HOW JAPANESE WORDS ARE PRONOUNCED

a as in *are*
e as in *when*
i as in *ea* of *eat*
o as in *not*
o as in *oh*
u as in *put*
ai as in *y* of *my*
ei as in *ay* of *day*

Other vowels, if together, are pronounced separately — Ieyasu (I-e-ya-su). Consonants are pronounced as in English, except that *g* is mostly hard, as in "go," never soft as in "gentry." Most syllables are evenly stressed. *Samurai* (sa-mu-rai): member of the warrior class of old Japan. *Shogun* (sho-o-gu-n): military ruler. Sometimes, as here, the vowel sound is doubled. *Kunsho* (kun-sho-o): medal.

JAPANESE NAMES

In Japan the family name is always put first, and then the personal name, for example, Minamoto Yoritomo. Minamoto was a clan name, while Yoritomo was a *shogun's* personal name. Tokugawa Ieyasu is the correct order to the Japanese eye and ear. "Ieyasu Tokugawa" would sound as odd to the Japanese as "Lincoln Abraham" would to us.

Many feminine personal names have the suffix *-ko*, which is written with the character for "child" — Hanako (flower-child) or Yuriko (lily-child). Many surnames describe the places at which people's ancestors lived, e.g. Matsushita which means "beneath the pine trees." Tanaka means "amid the rice-fields."

▼ The Ainu are a Caucasian people, and were the original inhabitants of Japan. As the Japanese gradually conquered the country, the Ainu were driven north, and now only a few thousand survive on Hokkaido. Their distinctive culture attracts many tourists to the north. The Ainu have pale skins and rounded eyes.

▼ Weddings are occasions for lavish displays of food and gifts. About half the guests will be friends from work. Men usually get married around the age of 28-30, while women marry younger, at about 24-26 years of age.

▼ Carp streamers — one for each boy in the family — are hung out on May 5, which is Boys' Day. The carp is renowned for its determination in swimming upstream, and is therefore thought to be a worthy example for boys to follow. Since 1945, a Girls' Day festival has also been set aside.

▲ Japanese do not of course all look alike: skin tone and facial features vary significantly from person to person. But all Japanese do have black hair and almond-shaped eyes. Over the last forty years they have tended to become taller and heavier, largely because of changes in diet.

11

From myth into history

The first Japanese immigrated from mainland Asia. When and how they arrived no one knows for certain. Archaeologists have identified a Jomon culture, dating from about 8000 BC. Jomon people lived by fishing and gathering and produced earthenware pottery with distinctive coiled patterns. Later migrants from China in about 350 BC brought a knowledge of the potter's wheel, of metal-working and of rice-growing. This Yayoi culture was followed by a so-called Tomb culture, which created Japan's first architecture.

In the fifth century AD the Yamato clan established its power in south central Honshu, around what is now Kyoto. The clan leader declared his descent from Jimmu Tenno, a legendary emperor of 660 BC who claimed to be a descendant of the sun goddess Amaterasu. The Yamato dynasty has reigned over Japan ever since.

Buddhism and the shoguns

During the sixth century AD Chinese influences brought Buddhism from India to Japan, along with a written script, theories about how government ought to be run and the idea that there should be a permanent capital. This was fixed first of all at Nara and then in AD 794 at nearby Kyoto which was known as Heiankyo. Elegant courtiers, devoted to poetry and the arts, dominated the culture of this Heian period. By the twelfth century the Yamato emperor was ruler in name only. He was still greatly respected but real power had passed out of the hands of courtiers and into those of *samurai* warriors. The most powerful *samurai* took the title of *shogun*, military dictator, and ruled in the emperor's name.

During the 1280s the Mongol conquerors of China twice tried to invade Japan, but their great invasion fleet was utterly destroyed by a massive storm.

MAIN EVENTS IN JAPANESE HISTORY

50,000 BC	Paleolithic culture.
8,000 BC	Jomon culture.
300 BC	Yayoi culture.
300 AD	Tomb culture.
400	Emergence of Yamato clan.
552	Introduction of Buddhism.
710–94	**Nara Period**
794–1159	**Heian Period.** Capital at Kyoto. *Samurai.*
1185–1333	**Kamakura Period.** Mongol threat.
1338–1549	**Ashikaga** or **Muromachi Period.** First European visits.
1568–1598	**Period of Unification.**
1600–1867	**Tokugawa Period.**
1867–1912	**Meiji Period.** Capital at Edo, renamed Tokyo, Modernization.
1894–5	Sino-Japanese War.
1912–1925	**Taisho Period.** Joins allies during Great War (1914–18).
1926	**Showa Period**
1941	Pearl Harbor: Japan enters World War II.
1945	Defeat of Japan.

▲ This wall painting of a Buddha is to be found at Horyuji temple, which is claimed as the oldest surviving group of wooden buildings in the world. Buddhism came to Japan via China from its home in India. The painting shows Indian influence.

▶ This Heian period (794–1185) scroll suggests the leisurely life of elaborately dressed courtiers, whose main amusements were poetry, calligraphy, gossip, and picnics. They had little contact with the ordinary world, and were known as "dwellers above the clouds."

▼ A thirteenth century scroll painting from the *Heike Monogatari* (Tales of the Heike Wars), which describes the power struggle between the Taira and Minamoto families. The illustration shows *samurai* warriors gathering around the elegant oxcart of a courtier.

▼ *The Tale of Genji,* written in about AD 1000 by a lady of the court named Murasaki Shikibu, is often held to be Japan's greatest literary work, despite the fact that its author, as a woman, would not have been regarded as a serious writer in her own times. This long novel tells of the amorous adventures of Prince Genji, who is a cultivated man of the court rather than a warrior or man of affairs. The skill of the novelist lies in her depiction of human moods and emotions and detailed descriptions of scenes and places, rather than dramatic action. Its pace and style are slow and elegant.

▲ A clay figure (*haniwa*) of a warrior, dating from the fourth century AD. These figures are found in burial mounds, which were erected over the bodies of tribal chiefs. Archaeologists have called this era the "Tomb Period."

13

Opening the closed country

The first westerners to visit Japan were Portuguese merchants who arrived in 1543. Missionaries soon followed and by the 1580s there were about 300,000 Christian converts in Japan. One reason for the rapid spread of the new faith was that Japan had been torn by civil wars for a century so there was no strong ruler to check outside influences.

The wars finally ended when Tokugawa Ieyasu beat all his rivals and took the title of *shogun* in 1603. He laid down the guidelines by which the Tokugawa family ruled for the next 250 years. The *shoguns* kept control of the main cities and highways, the silver mines and ports, about a quarter of all the land and the emperor himself. They kept the *daimyo* (feudal lords — literally "great names") under control by a network of spies, and by taking hostages.

The closed country

Ieyasu's successors strengthened his control system by closing the country to foreigners and stamping out Christianity. They feared another civil war in which Christian *daimyo* might get support from Christian foreigners. The only westerners allowed to trade with Japan were Protestant Dutch.

In 1853 an American squadron of modern steam-ships commanded by Commodore Perry arrived off Japan and demanded that the *shogun* open the country to trade. He had to agree and other westerners soon established themselves in Japan. Some *samurai* wanted to drive them out, and in 1868 they forced the *shogun* to resign and made the young emperor ruler of Japan. He called his reign "Meiji" (meaning "enlightened rule"). His supporters soon saw that the westerners were too strong to be driven out; so they set out to modernize Japan on western lines. Young men were sent to study abroad and western experts were brought to Japan to build up its industries. By 1894 Japan was strong enough to fight China for control of Korea. In 1904-5 she defeated Russia as well. By the time Emperor Meiji died in 1912, Japan was a world power.

▲ Osaka Castle, the last center of resistance to Tokugawa Ieyasu was stormed in 1615. Castles were built as headquarters for *daimyo*, and towns grew up around them. The *daimyo* controlled each region of Japan, but were regulated by the central authority of the *shoguns*.

▶ Saigo Takamori (1827–77) helped to lead the Meiji Restoration of 1868, but he then began to oppose the rapid westernization of the country because it disrupted the traditional ways of the peasants and *samurai*. He placed himself at the head of a hopeless rebellion in his native province of Satsuma, and was defeated in battle by Japan's new western-style army. Rather than surrender, he asked a friend to behead him on the battlefield. Japanese respect his unselfish loyalty to tradition, and a statue of the great Saigo stands in Tokyo's Ueno Park today.

▼ Japanese society during the Tokugawa Period was divided into four classes, according to the theory of the Chinese philosopher Confucius. At the top were the *samurai*, warrior-officials who governed the country. Leading *samurai* were known as *daimyo*. Next came the peasants, about 90 percent of the population. In theory they were highly valued because they grew crops for food. In practice, they were ruled harshly, although some did become prosperous. Artisans, or craftworkers, came third. Merchants were the least important group, according to the system, because they produced nothing directly. In practice, they were often rich and powerful, acting behind the scenes as financiers.

The four classes of Japanese society during the Tokugawa Period (1600-1867)

Samurai

Artisans (craftsmen)

Merchants

Peasants

▲ A textile factory. Cotton and silk were the first industries to mechanize, and provided major exports. Peasant women provided most of the labor, and were often exploited.

▼ Emperor Meiji, who presided over Japan's rapid modernization. He abolished the four-class system and in 1889 introduced a western-style constitution.

▶ Conscription was introduced in 1872 and *samurai* forbidden to wear swords in 1876. The new army was trained by German instructors.

▼ Japan on the road to becoming a great power. An aggressive foreign policy added neighboring territory to Japan, as China and Russia were defeated.

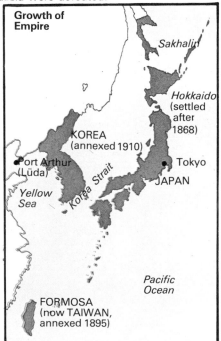

15

Japan emerges

Japan's status as a great power did not bring security, and the wealth from its new industries was not evenly shared. In 1925 all men were given the vote, but it was feared that discontent might lead to communist revolution.

The world depression of 1929–31 brought widespread unemployment and hunger to Japan. Democratic politicians seemed to have no cure for the country's problems. Right-wing extremists inside and outside the army pushed Japan toward an aggressive foreign policy. Their idea was to set up, by force, a secure trade area for Japan. By 1937 Japanese troops were engaged in a full-scale war in China. The army had taken over politics, although in theory the government was still answerable to the National Diet.

War and defeat
The fall of France in 1940 during World War II prompted Japan to invade France's colonies in Southeast Asia. Japan then attacked Hawaii and British colonies in Asia, drawing the United States and Great Britain into war in the Pacific. At first, Japanese forces were brilliantly successful, but in the long run Japan could not match the resources of its opponents and was forced to retreat from all its conquests. The Pacific war was a bitter one, but it ended in 1945, when the United States dropped atomic bombs on the Japanese cities of Hiroshima and Nagasaki.

Reform and rebirth
The American occupation (1945–52) gave Japan a new democratic constitution as well as reforms in education, agriculture, and industry. By 1955 the economy had returned to its prewar level. By 1970 Japan had become an economic superpower.

Japan's democratic government is headed by a prime minister and based on popular support. All Japanese over age 20 may vote. The country has more than 1,000 political parties, including active Communist and Socialist parties, but the Liberal Democratic party (LDP) has won most elections since 1955. This party favors economic stability and has the support of the business world.

◄ Emperor Hirohito (1901–89) as a young man. His reign spanned much of the 20th century and was marked by the end of Japan's expansionist ambitions and the country's emergence as an economic superpower. He became regent (ruling on behalf of his father) in 1921 and became emperor in 1926. He named his reign *Showa*, which means "Radiant Peace." The constitution adopted by Japan after World War II defines the emperor as a symbol of national unity, rather than an actual ruler, and Hirohito's role thereafter was ceremonial.

► The Shinjuku district of Tokyo, Japan's capital, is a crowded, lively center of shopping and entertainment that blazes with neon by night. Japanese cities recovered quickly from the devastation of war to become some of the most densely populated urban centers in the world.

▼ On December 7, 1941 a Japanese strike force made a surprise attack on the U.S. Naval base at Pearl Harbor, Hawaii. As an operation, it succeeded in inflicting great destruction. However, it also served to unite the American people in support of the war, and so ensured Japan's eventual defeat.

◄ Hiroshima, August 6, 1945. More than 100,000 people were killed outright by the world's first atomic bomb. Forty years later, survivors of the immediate blast were still dying from its effects. Today Hiroshima is a thriving city again, with nearly 900,000 inhabitants, but the terrible devastation will never be forgotten.

▲ Postwar Japanese life has been transformed by new technology and automation. The country now enjoys high living standards. Nevertheless, some Japanese fear that their society has paid a price for these innovations, and is losing touch with its traditional human values.

◄ Emperor Akihito and Empress Michiko (center) at home with their children. Although Akihito broke with tradition by marrying a woman who was not a member of the nobility, he is still honored by most Japanese as the living symbol of the nation's history and culture.

17

Japan's impact on the world

Many people around the world know Japan through its products with brand names such as Sony, Honda, and Canon. Japan is the world's largest producer of automobiles (7.9 million in 1990), televisions (14.2 million), and videocassette recorders (27.5 million). It is also the world's largest shipbuilder and the second overall producer, after the United States, of goods and services. This high industrial output is fueled by foreign oil. Japan is the world's biggest importer of energy, as it has almost no energy resources of its own. More than 95 percent of Japan's energy is imported, mostly in the form of petroleum from the Middle East.

In addition to appliances, high-technology equipment, and machines, Japan exports metals, textiles, and chemicals. Its imports, besides energy, include food, machinery, cotton and other fibers for the textile industry, and metal ores and scrap metal for the metalworking industry. Japan's principal trading partner is the United States. In 1990, the two countries began talks aimed at reducing the trade deficit between them by making it easier for U.S. companies to sell their products to Japanese consumers.

During the 1980s, Japanese firms invested in Europe, the United States, and Great Britain, where Japanese factories have been built in some older industrial regions. Japan is also the major economic force in Southeast Asia and has become a leading donor of economic aid and technical assistance to developing nations. The countries around the Pacific Rim are moving into greater international prominence, and Japan is the economic leader of the Pacific community.

Corporations and businesspeople from the United States and elsewhere have visited Japan to study the management techniques and business methods that have created the country's high productivity. At the same time, many Japanese study abroad to gain expertise in science and mathematics.

Culture and colonies
Japan's economic influence is new, but it has influenced the world in other ways. Western artists in the late 19th century were deeply impressed by Japanese painting, pottery, and metalwork, and this influence contributed to trends in western art. At the same time, books about Japan became extremely popular with western readers; one such book inspired Giacomo Puccini's popular opera *Madama Butterfly*.

Japan's victory over Russia in 1905 helped bring about the communist revolution in defeated Russia, and it also encouraged Asian nationalists in India and elsewhere to believe that an Asian people could overcome a western colonial power. And, although Japan's colonial rule in Korea and Taiwan was bitterly resented and often brutal, it did raise health and living standards. It also laid the foundation for the later economic success of those nations, just as its invasion of British, French, and Dutch colonies in Southeast Asia during World War II ended colonial rule in those lands.

◀ A camera store in Tokyo. Japanese high-technology products such as optical and electronic goods are known worldwide for their excellent design and reliability.

▲ The logo of Japan Air Lines, JAL was established as recently as 1954, but was the second airline in the world to establish around-the-world service. It is now the largest intercontinental passenger carrier, linking 45 cities in 30 countries.

▶ Japanese artists such as Ando Hiroshige (1797–1858) had a major impact on later western painters such as Whistler and Van Gogh. They admired his free and vigorously impressionistic style.

▶ Despite the language barrier, Japanese films have achieved a cult following in the west. This is a scene from *Yojimbo*, a comedy-thriller set in feudal times. Its director is Akira Kurosawa, one of Japan's most influential film makers.

▼ A Toyota parts distribution center in Great Britain. As Japan's home market for cars stabilizes and Japanese industry switches to making "hi-tech" products, an increasing proportion of Japanese manufacturing will be located overseas. Japanese cars have penetrated deeply into the United States market.

Religions and festivals

Most Japanese follow one of two religious traditions — Shinto or Buddhism. Large numbers also belong to what are called "new" religions, such as Tenrikyo or Soka Gakkai. These combine new interpretations of traditional beliefs with styles of worship and organization influenced by Christianity. There are about a million Christians in Japan. Freedom of religion is guaranteed by the constitution.

The "way of the gods"
Shinto, "the way of the gods," was born in Japan and is found nowhere else. It has no founder, no scriptures, no special day of worship. It demands reverence for nature and sincerity in human affairs. It has many festivals and ceremonies which celebrate happy events such as harvests, marriages, and births or the coming of a New Year. When the army controlled politics, Shinto was made into a form of emperor worship. The post-war constitution forbids state support of any religion.

Buddhism
Buddhism came from China in the sixth century and was taken up by the court. As it was adapted to Japanese ways it became popular with ordinary people. Later a particularly Japanese form of Buddhism — Zen — developed. Zen stressed self-discipline and appealed especially to *samurai*. In modern times it has attracted followers in western countries. Buddhism complements Shinto in many ways, having extensive scriptures and a moral code.

Festivals
Japan's two most important festivals mark the New Year and a mid-summer commemoration of the dead, known as O-Bon. Many regions and villages also have their own festivals, associated with the spring sowing or autumn harvest or some famous local event or Shinto god (*kami* — literally "superior").

At festival times it is customary to visit shrines and to exchange gifts. There are often very boisterous processions, and special foods are prepared and eaten. Many city families make a point of going back to visit their home village.

JAPANESE FESTIVALS AND HOLIDAYS	
January 1	New Year's Day
January 15	Adults' Day
February 3	Setsubun
February 11	National Accession Day (of Jimmu)
March 3	Girls' Day
March 20	Spring Festival
April 8	Buddha's Birthday
May 1	May Day
May 3	Constitution Day
May 5	Children's Day/ Boys' Day
July 7	Tanabata Star Festival
July 15	O-Bon (in cities)
August 15	O-Bon (in country)
September 15	Respect for the Aged Day
September 23	Autumn Festival
October 10	Sports Day
November 3	Culture Day
November 15	7-5-3 Festival
November 23	Labor Day

A red-painted *torii* (the literal meaning of which is "bird-perch") usually marks the entrance to a Shinto shrine. Like many others, this is set in an area of outstanding natural beauty, symbolizing the close association between Shinto and reverence for nature. It is not uncommon for Shinto shrines and Buddhist temples to exist side by side. Throughout history, Japan's two religious traditions have affected each other. Sometimes they have been in conflict, but they now coexist harmoniously.

▼ A Buddhist monk at worship. Buddhism preaches simplicity, but forms of worship and their settings are often notable for their magnificence. Buddhism in Japan is divided into more than a hundred different sects. More than 83 million Japanese identify themselves as members of one of these sects.

◄ Funerals are usually conducted according to Buddhist rites. The bodies are cremated and grave sites marked by a simple stone column. At O-Bon, in midsummer, families visit the graves, clean them and decorate them with flowers.

▲ The figure of the Buddha has inspired Japanese artists and craftworkers for more than a thousand years. This gigantic bronze figure is over 50 feet tall. It is housed at Nara, near Kyoto, in the largest wooden building in the world. It was completed in AD 794 and is now a major attraction for tourists as well as pilgrims.

◄ A portable shrine (*mikoshi*) is carried through the streets at a local village festival. The shrine represents the home of the *kami*, the local deity, who is believed to protect the surrounding area from evil influences.

Industry and crafts

The secret of Japan's postwar industrial success has been its ability to create new industries rapidly to meet the changing needs of international customers. Japan's first priority after the war was to build up its heavy industries, such as steelmaking and chemical production, on which other industries rely for their raw materials. Then the emphasis shifted to the industries that use those raw materials, such as shipbuilding, automaking, and plastics manufacturing. The world oil crises of the 1970s greatly increased the cost of imported energy, and this encouraged Japanese industry to increase the manufacture of high-technology goods such as electronic equipment, computers, and robots. These products require less energy to manufacture. An additional advantage is that high-technology industry generally causes less pollution than heavier industry, and Japan has acquired serious air and water pollution problems along with its prosperous industrial economy. Furthermore, high-technology industry has allowed Japan to make use of its best resources—a skilled and diligent work force.

Many people in the West have admired Japanese labor relations. The principal features of industrial relations in large corporations are lifetime employment, pay and promotion according to seniority, and worker participation in forming company plans and policies. Company uniforms, slogans, and outings build team spirit and loyalty to the corporation. Employees and their families are considered part of a hugh corporate family, and most people expect to work for the same company for their entire lives, instead of moving from company to company as is common in the United States and other industrialized nations. The larger Japanese companies provide vacation lodging, medical services, children's scholarships, subsidized housing, and social activities for their employees.

More than half of all Japanese, however, are employed by smaller firms that do not provide all these benefits. Although relations between workers and management are generally good, Japan does experience strikes—usually in April, when the new financial year begins.

Traditional skills

Japan's modern industries are based on a long tradition of skill in many crafts. The swords made for the *samurai* warriors, for example, have never been equalled; each blade is a painstaking combination of several steels with various degrees of hardness. Other traditional crafts include woodcarving, making rice paper, weaving silk cloth, creating lacquered cabinets or porcelain vases, and carving *netsuke*, small figures of jade or other precious substances that are attached to the sashes of traditional Japanese clothing. Artisans also create dolls dressed in elaborate traditional costumes of silk, lunchboxes woven of bark strips, painted paper lanterns and umbrellas, and bowls used for the *chanoyu*, or tea ceremony. Many Japanese incorporate these items into everyday life.

Traditional handicrafts are still alive in Japan, although some crafts have few practitioners and many items once made by hand are now produced in factories. Since 1955, the country's most gifted craftspeople have been named National Living Treasures. They receive funds from the country's Agency for Cultural Affairs so that they can continue to practice their crafts. The agency also provides scholarships for apprentices who wish to learn the traditional handicrafts from these master artisans. Many museums in Japan, as well as others throughout the world, contain examples of fine Japanese crafts.

▼ A factory making video-cassette recorders. Japan's highly successful electronics industry grew out of wartime production of radios for military use. Cameras and chemicals also had the same wartime origins. Today, however, Japan's chief market is not the military, but consumers, whether at home or overseas.

▲ Fishing fleets have traditionally relied on Japan's coastal waters, but rising demand and the pollution of coastal areas by uncontrolled industrial growth in the 1950s and 1960s have forced fishermen to operate as far away as the Indian Ocean.

▼ Japan began to mass-produce cars as recently as 1957. By 1980 Japan had surpassed the United States to become the world's largest producer. Toyota is the second largest car manufacturer in the world, and Nissan the fourth largest.

Traditional crafts

▲ A weaver using a traditional hand-loom. Today, computerized weaving is also possible, creating new variations on old themes.

▲ Handmade paper is still greatly valued for certain special uses, such as calligraphy, and making fans, lanterns, and screens.

▲ *Tatami,* the traditional floor-covering for homes and palaces alike, consists of woven rice-straw mats, bound at the edges. It is still essentially a handcrafted product.

Shopping with style

It is said that there is one store for every fourteen families in Japan. Most are very small, either mom and pop shops, run by retired couples and selling everyday necessities, or speciality shops, dealing in a single product, such as paper or neckties. Most are family businesses and all place great emphasis on courtesy and personal service. Even the smallest goods are carefully wrapped. Local shops rely on the same circle of families for their living and take trouble to provide just what they want. When it comes to food, and especially fish and vegetables, Japanese housewives like to shop daily and sometimes separately for every meal.

The distribution system provides work for about one-seventh of the entire labor force, through a complex chain of wholesalers and retailers. This may make goods more expensive to the customer in the end but it does mean they get exactly what they want. Supermarkets might be more efficient but their spread has been slowed down by organizations of small shopkeepers who have great political influence when they act together.

Department stores
The complex distribution system makes it difficult for an importer to get goods on the shelf of a neighborhood store. Foreign goods are much more likely to be found in a big city department store. The Japanese claim to have invented the department store back in the seventeenth century. It is certainly true that the giant firm of Mitsui can be traced back 300 years to a Tokyo draper's. A major *depato* like Mitsukoshi or Daimaru will not only sell everything from furniture to delicatessen but also have a restaurant and exhibition area. The "bargain basement" will often be on the top floor to encourage the customer to stop off at one of the other departments on the way up or down. Shops and stores tend to be especially busy just before the New Year and the midsummer O-Bon festival, which are the great annual occasions for gift-giving.

Most shopping is done by women. This is not only because the men are at work: women manage the family finances in four-fifths of all Japanese

▲ Department stores aim to give the customer the same style of personal service as a small shop. This means having a large staff, including not only sales assistants, but women who stand by the doors to bow at people entering and leaving the store. The goods for sale include traditional Japanese items as well as more modern things.

homes, and make most of the major spending decisions.

Shopping in Tokyo
As the nation's capital and largest city, Tokyo, not surprisingly, boasts the largest number of shops and department stores. Its most famous shopping area is probably the Ginza, where the leading *depato* are to be found; but other areas are also important. Asakusa, the district around the Kannon temple, dedicated to the Buddhist goddess of mercy, is where many wholesalers of traditional goods are located. Such traditional items include textiles, toys, fireworks, cheap china and lacquerware, and religious articles, such as shrines, drums and candlesticks. This clearly reflects the original character of the area, which catered to the needs of pilgrims visiting the temple.

A complete contrast is Akihabara, where all the latest electronic gadgets can be seen in the discount shops. This is one of the areas where a customer can hope to bargain over the price of something. Unlike most other Asian countries, Japan usually operates on a fixed price system: haggling is rare.

▼ Flowers and streamers decorate a new shop in celebration of its opening. Sometimes a priest from the local Shinto shrine will perform a special ceremony to assure the future prosperity of the new enterprise. Many everyday Japanese customs are bound up with Shinto beliefs.

▲ Japanese women usually control the family budget. Housewives often have the time as well as the knowledge to be very discriminating consumers.

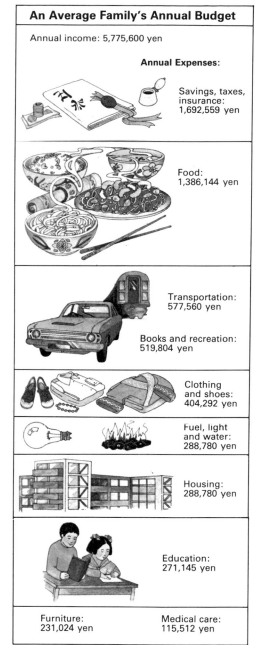

◀ Japanese currency is based on the *yen*, which in 1990 exchanged for about 140 to the US dollar or 226 to the pound sterling.

An Average Family's Annual Budget

Annual income: 5,775,600 yen

Annual Expenses:

Savings, taxes, insurance: 1,692,559 yen

Food: 1,386,144 yen

Transportation: 577,560 yen

Books and recreation: 519,804 yen

Clothing and shoes: 404,292 yen

Fuel, light and water: 288,780 yen

Housing: 288,780 yen

Education: 271,145 yen

Furniture: 231,024 yen

Medical care: 115,512 yen

▲ One major difference between the Japanese and many Western peoples is the high priority placed on saving in Japan. Most Japanese set a large percentage of income aside as savings and adjust their spending accordingly. Taxes are relatively low in Japan, but people expect to rely on their savings for a great part of the cost of their children's education and their own old-age income.

◀ Market scenes are more than a reminder of bygone days. Much daily shopping is still done at general street markets. Fish markets are to be found in every port, and in the largest cities there are specialized markets for such items as antiques and second hand books.

Town and country

Nearly 77 percent of all Japanese live in cities. More than half of the population lives in or near the four great cities of Tokyo, Osaka, Nagoya, and Kita-kyushu. Each of these has good access to trains, roads, and seaports, and each has a surrounding plain suitable for agriculture.

Tokyo
Unlike many of the world's great cities, Tokyo is not an ancient settlement. Five hundred years ago it was a fishing village called Edo. Then Tokugawa Ieyasu decided to make his headquarters there. He built a massive castle. By 1700, Edo had about a million inhabitants. In 1868, the emperor moved from Kyoto to Edo, and the city was renamed Tokyo, or "eastern capital." It had 8.3 million inhabitants in 1990.

Villages
Historically, most Japanese lived in villages, and many city dwellers still return to visit their ancestral homes and family graves at the time of the O-Bon festival. Most villages now have the modern conveniences of city life or are within easy reach of them.

Transportation
Japan's population centers are linked by an efficient transportation system. The first railway was opened in 1872, and railways remained the basis of transportation until after World War II. The super-fast bullet train service, inaugurated in 1964, links the major cities of Honshu and Kyushu islands. Roadbuilding has increased since the 1950s, and it is intended that by the end of the 20th century all the islands will be connected by bridges and tunnels. There were about 28.6 million private cars on the roads in 1990.

▲ Japanese village life. For most of their history, the Japanese people have been village dwellers, and even in an urban age traditional values persist.

◀ Window-shopping, or just strolling along busy streets, are cheap forms of amusement for city dwellers. On Sundays large areas are closed to traffic, forming a "pedestrian paradise."

▲ A six-lane urban highway. For many years rail was developed at the expense of roads, but today a network of highways links the nation.

▲ A visit to the nation's capital: a photographer records the moment outside the Imperial Palace, which lies at the heart of Tokyo.

◄ Rush hour is squash hour! Two scientists at Tokyo University worked out that the average commuter has already used up half a day's energy by the time that he or she arrives at work. The railway employs people to push the passengers into the cars.

▼ Commuting is a way of life in Japan. More than 10% of the entire labor force has a journey of more than one hour each way in order to arrive at work. Around Tokyo the proportion rises to 25%. Whole districts are centered upon important commuter stations such as Shinjuku.

▲ The Ginza is by day a major shopping area, and by night an entertainment district, with 1,500 bars within a radius of half a mile. The word *ginza* refers to the mint which opened here in 1612.

The family bond

Traditional Japanese society was based on the extended family system. The eldest male, as head of the household, had immense power over its members and this power was backed up by law. His wife reigned supreme in domestic affairs. Her authority was symbolized by the large wooden spoon she used to dole out the rice at mealtimes. The least powerful adult was the youngest daughter-in-law, who was usually also the hardest worked. Among the children, boys were indulged, while girls were trained from the earliest years to be submissive and helpful around the house. Great respect was always shown to the aged.

Reform
The 1946 Constitution abolished the old laws which gave fathers such authority and decreed that the family property should pass to the eldest son on the death of the head of the household. Now all adults are equal before the law and men and women have the same rights in marriage, divorce, and inheritance.

In practice men and women in Japan live rather separate lives. Men leave home early to go to work and often work late or go out for the evening with workmates or clients. Women have the main responsibility, not only for running the home but also for making the major decisions about the children's education.

The only time when the whole family can be sure of being together is on Sunday, when they will go to the park or the beach, or into the countryside. Sometimes men have to work away from their families in other parts of Japan or abroad. These "business bachelors" are an increasingly common phenomenon, as indeed are working wives. Respect for the aged remains strong. But it is rather difficult for couples living in small city apartments to find space for aged parents as well.

▼ A family meal, but father is absent. Sunday is usually the only day the whole family can be sure of being together.

▼ Traditional finery, but attitudes have changed. The modern family is smaller and more self-contained.

◄ Today most Japanese families have their own bathroom, but despite this the public bath-house remains a popular place to meet and gossip, especially in rural and resort areas. Soap is never used in the bath itself. People soap and rinse themselves outside the bath, then get in to soak and relax. The Shinto religion has always placed great emphasis on the notion of purity.

▲ A room in a traditional house. Pressure on living space encouraged the Japanese to keep furniture to a minimum and use each room for several different purposes. Bedding was stored in a cupboard by day, and the bedroom thus became available for use as a living room at other times. Note the straw mats on the floor (*tatami*) and the sliding doors.

◄ Many families live in apartment blocks (*danchi*) which they rent from companies or local authorities. The typical apartment is usually a "2DK" — two rooms and an eat-in kitchen, together with a bathroom and, sometimes a balcony. This is adequate for a small family — but there's not much room for grandmother.

▲ Reverence before the family altar. Many surviving religious ceremonies are associated with the cycle of family life, marking the great occasions of birth, marriage, and death.

▲ Mother and child enjoy the fun of the fair. Children often spend more time with their mother than with their father.

▶ Father and son play *pachinko* or pinball. Long office hours and socializing after work leave little time for fathers to enjoy the company of their children. Nevertheless, family ties are very close.

Japanese cooking

Rice is the staple food of Japan and is eaten with every meal. The word for breakfast literally means "morning rice." The Japanese prefer their rice to be rather sticky; this makes it easier to eat with chopsticks (*hashi*). Rice is also used to make *sake*, the traditional alcoholic drink of Japan. *Sake* should be warmed and drunk at body temperature. It is often drunk at festivals as well as with food.

Fish

Fish provides the main source of protein in Japan. It is eaten raw as well as cooked and processed into various kinds of pastes and fishcakes. Another source of protein is *tofu*, a sort of blancmange-like substance made from soybeans; it is eaten on its own or in soup with vegetables.

New foods

Since the American Occupation the Japanese have come to eat far more western foods and especially meat and dairy products. But there is still a major difference between the generations. Younger people will happily eat cheese or drink coffee. But older people tend to stick to a traditional diet of rice, fish, vegetables, and green tea.

Eating out is an important part of Japanese social life. Chinese, Korean, and Italian restaurants are popular. *Sushi* bars, serving tasty and savory rice snacks, are very popular with businessmen.

Health

The traditional Japanese diet is a very healthy one, being low in fats, yet still adequately provided with proteins from fish, eggs, and vegetables. As a result, Japan has one of the lowest rates of heart disease among the industrial countries.

Presentation

Japanese meals, even the simplest, are always beautifully presented. Skilled chefs not only slice up fish and meat with precision into bite-sized portions, but also carve vegetables and pickles into decorative accompaniments.

▲ Businessmen often eat their evening meal in a restaurant, together with their colleagues and clients. This can be a leisurely affair, allowing ample time for business negotiations and social conversation. Lunch, by contrast, is often rather a hurried business, which has to fit into a crowded schedule.

▲ When it comes to buying food, Japanese consumers are faced with a bewildering variety of choice. Modern methods of preservation and packaging mean that favorite foodstuffs are now available all year long. Pickled fish, meat, and vegetables are essential for every Japanese meal.

▲ A *yudofu* set meal. *Tofu* (bean curd) is used as a component of many Japanese meals. It provides a high protein content, and has in recent years become popular as a health food throughout the world. The Japanese diet is a very healthy one, with natural methods of preservation, such as fermentation, preferred to artificial ones.

► The presentation of food is very important. Each item is arranged artistically on the dish.

▲ *Yakitori* is a very popular food: grilled chicken skewered on bamboo. It is served in the open air and is often drunk with *sake*.

A DAY'S MENU
Traditional breakfast
Miso (bean curd) soup, rice, raw egg, pickled vegetables, green tea, grilled fish, salad.

Lunch
Curries or noodles, side salad, beer, *or*
O-bento (packed lunch box) containing cold rice, pickles, omelette, breaded fried pork, packet of soy sauce.

Dinner
Tempura — fresh prawns, white fish, and green vegetables, fried in a light batter — and hot *sake*, *or*
Nabe-monu — stew of meat or seafood with bean curd and vegetables, cooked in an earthenware pot. Popular in winter.

► Garnishes are an essential part of Japanese cooking. Vegetables are often cut or sliced into floral designs; here, the white radish has been carved into a chrysanthemum shape.

Schools and examinations

Since the 19th century, Japan has had a high literacy rate. Today that rate is nearly 100 percent; almost all Japanese over the age of 15 can read and write. The country's educational system is modern and well equipped. Each year, Japan spends more than 9 percent of its national budget on education. It has 25,000 primary schools, 17,000 junior high and secondary schools, 600 vocational schools and junior colleges, and more than 400 universities. Education in the sciences is emphasized at Tsukuba Science City, a collection of two universities and many research laboratories built in the 1970s. Other educational "cities" are under construction.

High standards

Japanese education is free and compulsory between the ages of 6 and 15. Most Japanese children, however, start school with a three-year kindergarten program that begins at age 3. At age 6 they enter primary school. There they study the same subjects as most students in western schools, but with special emphasis on mathematics and science. English is taught in all schools and most children study it because they must pass a written test in English to enter college. One of the most challenging subjects, however, is the Japanese language, which has the world's most complex writing system. Basic literacy requires mastering two forms of phonetic script and nearly 2,000 *kanji*, or Chinese characters, which have been used in Japanese writing since 400 AD. Many students also take classes in traditional Japanese arts and crafts such as flower arranging or calligraphy.

Between ages 12 and 15, students attend junior high school. Although they are allowed by law to drop out of school at age 15, few young people do so. More than 95 percent of them continue their education. They may attend three years of secondary school between ages 15 and 18 or five years of technical school between ages 15 and 20. Those who go to secondary school may then attend junior college or university.

Education is highly valued in Japan. Parents feel that their children's education is the key to a good future, so they spend much money on tuition at the *juku,* or cramming schools, that students attend in the evenings to help them prepare for tests. Most young people have three hours or more of homework every day—twice as much on the weekends. Tests are difficult at all levels. The examinations that students must pass to enter college are fiercely competitive, and the struggle to get into a good college creates what the Japanese call "examination hell."

Japan's educational standards are very high, and its young people perform better on exams than those of most other countries. Yet some Japanese educational reformers worry that the testing system puts too much pressure on students. They would like creativity and individual interests to receive greater encouragement in the schools.

▲ A secondary-school student in Hiroshima takes lecture notes. If she intends to go to college, she will soon face a series of extremely difficult entrance examinations.

▲ Primary school pupils at work on a project. Many children go to a kindergarten or playgroup before starting formal education at the age of 6. The emphasis is still on reading, writing, and arithmetic. By the time they are twelve they must have mastered nearly 900 of the Chinese characters with which Japanese is written. Only a small minority of Japanese primary schools are private. Great importance is attached to the teaching of the young, and educational standards are generally high.

▼ Junior high school pupils follow a broad curriculum, which is set down by the Ministry of Education. The Ministry also has to approve all school textbooks. Everyone must learn English, which is Japan's first foreign language. Modern teaching aids are readily available, and a strong emphasis is placed on the teaching of mathematics, shown below.

▲ Schoolgirls on an outing to a shrine. School trips are thought to promote friendship among pupils and loyalty to the school as well as helping pupils to appreciate the national heritage. Pupils are encouraged to save for school trips years beforehand; this is intended to get them used to thinking for the long term. These girls are wearing the standard uniform.

▼ A university lecture hall. Japan has over 400 universities, and the leading ones rank among the best in the world. Top companies recruit their management employees from these colleges, so competition for entrance into them is very intense. Students who manage to get a place have proved their ability, and can look forward to a secure career.

Nature into art

Art and nature are almost inseparable in Japanese culture. the country's dramatic scenery of mountain and valley, rocks and waterfalls, forests and plains has inspired generations of poets, painters, and craftworkers.

Art and design

Certain characteristics of Japanese art stand out as being clearly related to the particular qualities of the country itself. One is a preference for natural materials and natural processes. The aged timbers of a house may be deliberately left unpainted as they turn gray and the stone lantern in a garden may be allowed to acquire a covering of moss and lichen. Old temple bells of bronze likewise develop a deep patina as the centuries pass. Another characteristically Japanese idea is that beauty is essentially fleeting, something that can be glimpsed but never grasped. Dew and mist, recurrent features of Japan's damp climate, symbolize this quality of impermanence for poet and painter alike.

Economy and spareness are also notable features of Japanese creativity and have passed into the country's modern industrial design. Japanese products are renowned worldwide for being smaller, lighter, thinner, and altogether more compact than those of other nations. Japanese painters have similarly been able to sketch a whole forest with half a dozen brush strokes. A potter may scratch four or five lines on a bowl or plate and suggest a bridge over a flowing river.

What could be more compact than that most characteristic of Japanese art-forms — the *haiku*? A poem of 17 syllables, arranged in just three lines, the *haiku* is a snapshot of a place, a person, or an event.

However, if the Japanese have carried nature into art, they have also brought art into nature. Gardening is one of the most favored of Japanese pastimes. Shrubs, stones, and water, rather than flowers as such, provide the main elements of a Japanese garden, which is as much a work of art as the house.

▼ The *Noh* drama is more than 600 years old. Originally an entertainment which was strictly for aristocrats, it never had to simplify its traditions for a popular audience. It has kept elaborate, stylized gestures, and complex, formal speech. A more popular form of drama developed from the seventeenth century onward. It appealed to town dwellers of the Tokugawa Period, and is still quite popular today. Known as *Kabuki*, it makes use of brilliant costumes. *Noh* actors wear masks and make slow gestures, but *Kabuki* actors wear make-up for action-packed dramas.

▲ A spring outing under boughs of cherry blossoms. The Japanese countryside and its changing seasons have been a major source of inspiration for artists and poets.

▶ The graceful, elegant lines of Daigoji Buddhist temple at Kyoto. Japanese architects have always aimed to make buildings harmonize with their natural setting, rather than dominate it. Perhaps the fact that wood rather than stone has always been the major building material has helped to keep this awareness alive. This pagoda shows Chinese influence.

▼ An early Buddhist sculpture in bronze, showing strong Chinese influence in its style. Japanese artists later developed their own characteristic styles, working in such materials as stone, wood, and ivory.

▲ This wood-block print is one of a series of *Thirty-six Views of Mount Fuji* by the great artist Hokusai (1760–1849), who called himself "the old man mad about drawing."

Multi-colored wood-block printing began in the mid-eighteenth century with the production of cheap souvenirs, but it soon became an art form.

▼ The Japanese style of flower arrangement, known as *ikebana*, is a perfect example of how the Japanese take natural objects as the starting point for forms of art. Other examples include the growing of miniature trees (*bonsai*).

Vacations and leisure

Most people probably associate the Japanese with hard work — and they do work hard. However they also know how to enjoy themselves. As in other modern countries, the leisure industry is a big business in itself. Nevertheless, traditional forms of amusement also survive.

Amusements and evening classes
Every Japanese home has television: indeed, 50% of the homes have two sets. The most popular programs are quiz shows, soap operas, and *samurai* dramas, but there are also many cultural and educational programs. Other home amusements include board games like *go*, a subtle contest of strategy; *shogi*, the Japanese form of chess; and *mah jong*, a Chinese gambling game.

Many Japanese work at their leisure and attend regular classes to achieve mastery of such traditional arts as calligraphy and the tea ceremony, or playing a musical instrument. Most people learn a little about these things at school, and many then take a more serious interest in them as adults.

Vacations
Japanese usually take short vacation breaks of two or three days, rather than the two or three weeks common in western countries. Hot spring resorts in the mountains are popular, as are trips to the beach. Employees of big firms often stay in hotels or lodges owned by their company. Vacationers can also stay at a *ryokan*, a traditional sort of inn, where the service is especially attentive and all the food and furnishings are in a Japanese style.

Many vacations are taken at times of major festivals, such as the Gion festival held in Kyoto in July, which celebrates the ending of a major epidemic 1100 years ago. Kyoto alone receives 20 million visitors a year: they visit its temples, parks, museums, and thousand shrines.

Tourism is growing rapidly. In 1983 just over one million foreign tourists came to Japan, and more than four million Japanese went overseas. The most popular destinations for Japanese tourists include Hawaii and Korea.

▼ Some games are only played at special times of the year. Here, girls in traditional dress play a New Year's card game. Quotes are matched with ancient poems printed on the cards. The game is called *utagaruta*.

▼ Not all Japanese pastimes require careful concentration and long training: devotees of *pachinko* (pinball) do however claim that it really is a test of one's skill. It certainly appeals to all ages and types of people.

▶ Nara, near Kyoto, is popular with daytrippers and tourists, who are attracted by its ancient temples and its famous deer. In the eighth century this was the capital of Japan.

▲ Fireworks are an ancient Chinese invention. In Japan, spectacular displays often round off many popular festivals.

◀ Japan's mountainous landscape provides abundant opportunities for winter sports such as skating, skiing, and climbing.

▶ The Japanese tea ceremony (*chanoyu*) began with the taking of tea by monks trying to keep up their concentration during long hours of meditation. It was formalized in the fifteenth century by Senno-Rikyu and has since been developed by masters of the art into many different schools. A full tea ceremony is performed in a special house, set apart in a garden. It requires the use of treasured utensils and the preparation of special snacks. Lasting several hours, it celebrates courtesy, hospitality, and beauty.

Sports and martial arts

The traditional sports of Japan evolved from the battlefield and the hunt. Fencing, archery, and various forms of unarmed combat enabled warriors to keep in trim and perfect their skills at the same time. Over the centuries, outstanding exponents of these arts founded schools of their disciples to teach their methods. These schools developed their own distinctive styles, rituals, and beliefs.

In postwar Japan, universities and police formed clubs of enthusiasts, and these played a leading part in maintaining interest in the martial arts. At the same time many traditional Japanese sports have become popular overseas.

Sumo

As far as spectators are concerned, the most popular of the traditional sports is *sumo* wrestling, which may date back 2,000 years or so. It has certainly been a professional sport for over two centuries. Six 15-day tournaments a year are held annually in Tokyo and the big cities. Successful champions are national heroes and major television personalities.

Judo

Judo — "the way of gentleness" — is a native Japanese sport which has acquired a following that is truly worldwide. Judo gained popularity in the United States after World War II. The first international *judo* championships were held in Japan in 1956, and it became an Olympic sport when Japan hosted the games in 1964.

Western sports

Since Japan opened its doors to the west, a number of new sports have been introduced, such as baseball, gymnastics, and tennis. Because leisure space is at a premium in crowded Japan, sports which require a large playing area, such as golf, tend to be very expensive. There are less than 1,400 golf courses in Japan for an estimated ten million golfers. Most people have to make do with a golf driving range. Sports which can be played on a small area, like volleyball, or on hard surfaces instead of grass, like tennis, tend to be more popular.

For young people, schools offer many sports facilities: gymnasiums, swimming pools, tennis and volleyball courts, baseball fields, and also *judo* halls.

▲ *Sumo* wrestlers weigh around 300 pounds and follow special exercise programs to strengthen their back, leg, and stomach muscles. The rules are actually simple, though the techniques are complex. The wrestlers poise themselves on either side of a ring bounded by a plaited straw rope. Often they strew salt around the ring, an ancient ritual of purification. Then they crouch down and size each other up, choosing the exact split-second in which to launch their assault. The action is usually over in a few seconds. Whoever is thrown out of the ring, or touches the ground with any part of his body other than his feet is declared the loser.

◄ Baseball was introduced from the United States more than a century ago, and ranks with *sumo* in its popularity as a spectator sport. There are professional teams, but there is also nationwide interest in the annual high-school tournament. Many companies have teams which play local league softball.

◄ Japanese archers use an asymmetrical bow and sometimes fire from a sitting position. Like the other martial arts, archery is a pursuit which demands mastery of technique and close mental concentration as well as physical effort. As such, it is regarded as a form of spiritual teaching as much as a sport. Calmness of spirit and self-discipline of character as well as physical well-being are expected to result from training.

▼ *Kendo*, the Japanese form of fencing, grew out of the practice techniques developed by *samurai* who wanted to stay in shape during the long centuries of peace under Tokugawa rule. The "swords" are made of bamboo, but it is still necessary to wear body armor and padding. Like *judo, kendo* is taught in schools, and there are many clubs of enthusiastic amateurs. Immediately after the war, the sport lost its popularity because many people associated it with military training. However this attitude has now changed, and its popularity has revived. *Kendo* has also begun to become popular abroad, and is now an international sport.

Judo, the "gentle way"

Judoka (people who take part in *judo*) wear different colored belts according to their level of skill. White is the lowest grade; black is the highest.

White belt
Yellow belt
Orange belt
Green belt
Blue belt
Brown belt
Black belt

A ninth or tenth dan in costume

Facing the future

Japan's postwar history has been one of success. A strong and stable democracy has been firmly established. The people enjoy a high standard of living and the world's longest life expectancy. Crime rates are low, and economic productivity is high.

The price of progress

The country has paid a price for its economic success. Much environmental damage has occurred, especially during the period of rapid industrialization between 1952 and 1973. Pollution remains a serious problem. The islands are densely populated, land is very expensive, and most living space is cramped. Roads and other facilities can barely meet the public's needs. Some Japanese are beginning to question their country's emphasis on progress and productivity and its use of land and resources.

One major difficulty is a byproduct of modern improvements in health care. Life expectancy has increased dramatically since World War II, to an average of 79 years. Japanese society is aging, and there is great concern about how to provide adequate pensions and health care for the ever-increasing elderly part of the population.

On the world stage

As one of the world's major economic powers, Japan is expected to take a leading role in international affairs. The Japanese do not always find this easy to do. A long history of isolation, together with geographic distance from the western nations, has made Japan slow to emerge as a world leader.

Yet the growing prosperity and importance of the Pacific Rim nations is thrusting Japan into the international limelight. New trade agreements and increased aid to developing nations are two ways in which Japan is working to cement its relations with other countries. Further efforts, such as participation in the environmental movement, will enhance Japan's role in international affairs.

▲ Japan's rapidly aging society presents new challenges in the provision of adequate medical and welfare services.

◀ Postwar Japan has seen occasional periods of political unrest with demonstrations from both the left and right. For the most part, political and industrial disputes have been conducted in an orderly manner.

▼ Like Great Britain, Japan operates a system of government in which a team of ministers, headed by the Prime Minister, makes policy. It is answerable to a National Diet. The ruling Liberal Democratic Party is in effect an alliance of personal factions, and the Prime Minister is usually the leader of the largest faction within the party. Faction leaders reward followers with jobs and funds in return for votes. Here, the cabinet faces the cameras.

▲ Not all Japanese technology is miniaturized! This is the world's largest television screen, at the city of Tsukuba. The world's smallest TV is also Japanese.

▼ Currency dealing: the *yen* is now a major world currency, and the Japanese stock exchange has been opened up to foreign firms.

▲ Tsukuba, 35 miles from Tokyo, has been established as a new "science city." It is intended to house more than forty government-funded National Research Institutes alongside a population of about 250,000. It is hoped that Tsukuba will be a planning ground for the new technologies of the 1990s.

Fast facts

Area 145,883 square miles (377,835 square kilometers)

Highest point Mount Fuji, 12,395 feet (3,756 meters)

Principal mountain ranges Japan Alps, Kitami, Kidaka, Kitakami, Abukama, Shikoku, Kyushu

Principal rivers Ishakari, Shinano, Tone

Population 123 million (in 1990)

Capital Tokyo

Other principal cities Yokohama, Osaka, Nagoya, Kitakyushu, Sapporo, Kobe, Hiroshima, Kyoto

Population density 844 people per square mile, 326 per square kilometer

Population distribution 77 percent urban, 23 percent rural

Ethnic composition 99.4 percent Japanese, 0.5 percent Korean, 0.1 percent Chinese

Language Japanese

Religion 90 percent of the population professes Shinto (a body of traditional beliefs and practices), 76 percent combines Buddhism with Shintoism, 9 percent has adopted "new religions" that combine various faiths, 1 percent is Christian

Average life expectancy 82 years for women, 76 for men

Land use 67 percent forests, 13 percent farmland, 2 percent meadows and pastures, 18 percent settlement and other uses

Employment of work force 48 percent in service industries; 33 percent in manufacturing, mining, and construction; 8 percent in agriculture and fishing; 11 percent in other, including government employees

Principal manufactured products Automobiles, appliances and electronic consumer goods, textiles, chemicals, steel, ships, machinery

Principal agricultural products Rice, potatoes, sugar beets, oranges, radishes, cabbages, onions, pork

Principal exports Electronic goods, automobiles, ships, appliances, steel, chemicals, scientific and optical equipment

Principal imports Petroleum, food, chemicals, textiles, metal ores and scrap

Currency The *yen* is the basic unit, divided into 100 *sen*; 140 yen equal 1 U.S. dollar, 226 yen equal 1 pound sterling (1990)

Head of government Prime minister

Formal chief of state Emperor

Form of government Constitutional monarchy with a two-chamber legislature called the National Diet

REGION	PREFECTURE	CAPITAL
Chubu	Aichi	Nagoya
	Fukui	Fukui
	Gifu	Gifu
	Ishikawa	Kanazawa
	Nagano	Nagano
	Niigata	Niigata
	Shizuoka	Shizuoka
	Toyama	Toyama
	Yamanashi	Kofu
Chugoku	Hiroshima	Hiroshima
	Okayama	Okayama
	Shimane	Matsue
	Tottori	Tottori
	Yamaguchi	Yamaguchi
Hokkaido	Hokkaido	Sapporo
Kanto	Chiba	Chiba
	Gumma	Maebashi
	Ibaraki	Mito
	Kanagawa	Yokohama
	Saitama	Urawa
	Tochigi	Utsunomiya
Kinki	Hyogo	Kobe
	Mie	Tsu
	Nara	Nara
	Shiga	Otsu
	Wakayama	Wakayama
Kyushu	Fukuoka	Fukuoka
	Kagoshima	Kagoshima
	Kumamoto	Kumamoto
	Miyazaki	Miyazaki
	Nagasaki	Nagasaki
	Oita	Oita
	Saga	Saga
Ryukyu	Naha	Okinawa
Shikoku	Ehime	Matsuyama
	Kagawa	Takamatsu
	Kochi	Kochi
	Tokushima	Tokushima
Tohoku	Akita	Akita
	Aomori	Aomori
	Fukushima	Fukushima
	Iwate	Morioka
	Miyagi	Sendai
	Yamagata	Yamagata

URBAN PREFECTURES

Kyoto
Osaka
Tokyo

Chronology

8000 BC — Japan's first culture, the Jomon culture, begins to form. The Jomon people build small settlements and produce distinctive pottery.

300 BC — The Yayoi culture brings influences from China, including rice farming, metalworking, and the potter's wheel.

300 AD — The Tomb culture creates Japan's first architecture and buries its rulers in immense earthen mounds.

400 AD — The Yamato, one of many rival clans, gains power in Kyushu and founds the imperial dynasty that still reigns in Japan.

405 — Chinese characters are introduced and used to write the Japanese language.

552 — Buddhism and Confucianism enter Japan from China.

710–794 — The imperial capital is at Nara. Some of Japan's first literary classics are written.

794–1159 — The imperial capital is at Heian (modern Kyoto). The *samurai,* or warrior, class emerges and grows powerful. Tea is introduced by Zen Buddhist monks from China and becomes the national beverage.

1192 — After several years of warfare, the Minamoto clan establishes the first shogunate, a government by military leaders.

late 13th century — The Mongol rulers of China twice try to invade Japan. Both attempts fail.

14th–15th centuries — Various shoguns, or military chiefs, vie for power.

1543 — The first European visitors—Portuguese traders—reach Japan.

late 16th century — Civil war ends and the country is unified by several powerful shoguns.

1600 — The Tokugawa shogunate is established. Japan is isolated from the rest of the world. Few foreigners are permitted to enter the country.

1853 — Commodore Matthew Perry of the United States Navy forces Japan to open its doors to western trade and diplomacy.

1867 — The capital is moved to Edo, which is renamed Tokyo. The modernization of Japan begins under Emperor Meiji.

1904–5 — Japan and China go to war. Japan wins Korea.

1904–5 — Japan and Russia go to war. Japan's mainland territory expands.

1926 — Hirohito becomes emperor.

1930s — After invading northern China, Japan is embroiled in war on the mainland.

1941 — Japan attacks Pearl Harbor, Hawaii, and the United States enters World War II.

1945 — The United States drops atomic bombs on Hiroshima and Nagasaki. Japan concedes defeat in World War II.

1945–52 — Japan is occupied by U.S. forces. A new constitution is introduced, along with economic, social, and political reforms.

1960s — A program of rapid industrialization causes economic productivity to surpass prewar levels.

1970s — Worldwide oil price increases bring about a shift to high-technology industry, at which Japan soon excels.

1989 — Hirohito dies. His son Akihito becomes emperor.

1990 — Japan and the United States negotiate to improve the balance of trade between the two nations.

Gazetteer

Japan has four main islands: Hokkaido, Honshu, Kyushu, and Shikoku. The name of the island on which a town is situated is given just after the name of the town. Population figures are for the year 1989.

Akita Honshu (39 45N 140 6E) Pop. 300,000. Port, exports petroleum.

Asahikawa Hokkaido (43 50N 142 20E) Pop. 364,000. *Sake,* wood products, textiles.

Chiba Honshu (35 40N 140 6E) Pop. 815,000. Steel manufacturing, paper, textiles.

Fujiyama (Mount Fuji) (35 30N 139 0E) Japan's highest mountain, on Honshu. A volcanic crater 12,395 ft. high, which last erupted in 1707. Sacred to the Shinto religion and famous for its beauty.

Fukuoka Kyushu (33 36N 130 27E) Capital of FUKUOKA PREFECTURE. Pop. 1,200,000. Exports porcelain and machinery. Manufactures textiles, chemicals, pottery, metal products.

Gifu Honshu (35 27N 136 46E) Capital of GIFU PREFECTURE. Pop. 409,000. Light industry, parasols, fans, lanterns, textiles, cutlery. Fishing center. Tourist resort.

Hamamatsu Honshu (34 42N 137 42E) Pop. 527,000. Manufacturing of motorcycles, pianos, organs, cloth, chemicals.

Himeji Honshu (34 50N 134 40E) Pop. 453,000. Famous castle. Manufacture of textiles, chemicals, leather goods.

Hiroshima Honshu (34 23N 132 27E) Capital of HIROSHIMA PREFECTURE. Pop. 1 million. On August 6, 1945, the first atomic bomb to be used in warfare was dropped here. The city was rebuilt and today is a seaport and industrial center.

Hokkaido Island (43 30N 143 0E) Pop. 6 million. Most northerly of the four main islands and very mountainous. Separated from Honshu by the Tsugaru Strait. The coldest of the islands, Hokkaido is foggy and heavily forested. Forestry, coalfields, fishing, agriculture. About 15,000 Ainu live here. The island was settled by the Japanese in the 16th century.

Honshu Island (36N 139E) Pop. 96 million. Includes 34 of Japan's 46 prefectures, and most of the important towns. Largest island, separated from Hokkaido by the Tsugaru Strait, from Shikoku by the Inland Sea and from Kyushu by the Kanmon Channel.

Kagoshima Kyushu (31 48N 130 40E) Capital of KAGOSHIMA PREFECTURE. Pop. 535,000. Minor seaport near the volcano Sakurajima. Manufacture of textiles and metal goods.

Kanazawa Honshu (36 35N 136 38E) Capital of ISHIKAWA PREFECTURE. Pop. 437,000. Manufacture of textiles, machinery, porcelain, lacquerware.

Kawasaki Honshu (35 4N 139 35E) Pop. 1,142,000. Shipbuilding, engineering. Manufacture of steel and textiles.

Kitakyushu Kyushu (33 52N 130 45E) Pop. 1,040,000. City formed in 1963 by the union of Moji, Kokura, Tobara, Yawata, and Wakamatsu. Center of industry.

Kobe Honshu (34 45N 135 12E) Capital of HYOGO PREFECTURE. Pop. 1,447,000. Port, extending for over 8 miles along coast of Osaka Bay. Exports ships, metal goods, textiles.

Kumamoto Kyushu (32 40N 130 45E) Capital of KUMAMOTO PREFECTURE. Pop. 570,000. Textiles, food processing. 16th century castle.

Kyoto Honshu (35 0N 135 30E) Capital of KYOTO PREFECTURE. Pop. 1,474,000. Famous for its crafts, porcelain, lacquer ware, dolls, fans, silk goods, brocades. Manufacture of machinery, textiles, chemicals. Center of Buddhist religion. Important tourist center, with many fine temples. Former imperial palace.

Kyushu Island (32 30N 131 0E) Pop. 15 million. Southernmost of the four main islands. Mountainous: volcanic Mt. Aso and hot springs.

Nagasaki Kyushu (32 45N 129 52E) Capital of NAGASAKI PREFECTURE. Pop. 447,000. Seaport, exporting coal, cement, tinned fish. Shipbuilding, engineering. Nagasaki was the only Japanese port open to foreign trade in the 16th century. On August 9, 1945, the world's second atomic bomb ruined the city.

Nagoya Honshu (35 17N 137 0E) Capital of AICHI PREFECTURE. Pop. 2,147,000. Seaport, Japan's fourth largest city. Manufacture of machinery, porcelain, textiles, chemicals.

Naha Okinawa (26 10N 127 40E) Pop. 305,000. Seaport and largest city on SW coast. Seat of local government. Exports sugar, dried fish. Manufactures chemicals, machinery, textiles.

Niigata Honshu (37 58N 139 2E) Capital of NIIGATA PREFECTURE. Pop. 483,000. Chief seaport on W coast of Honshu. The harbor is unsheltered and prone to silting. Export of oil, fertilizers. Manufacture of chemicals, machinery, textiles.

Okayama Honshu (34 40N 133 54E) Capital of OKAYAMA PREFECTURE. Pop. 587,000. Port. Manufacture of agricultural implements, cotton goods, porcelain.

Okinawa Island (26 30N 128 0E) Largest of the Ryukyu Islands. Pop. 1,250,000. Sugar cane, sweet potatoes, rice. The scene of heavy fighting during World War II. USA returned Okinawa to Japanese control in 1972.

Osaka Honshu (34 40N 135 39E) Capital of OSAKA PREFECTURE. Pop. 2,645,000. Seaport exporting textiles, machinery, metal goods. Manufacture of steel, chemicals, cement. Many cotton mills. Many Buddhist and Shinto temples. 16th century castle.

Ryukyu Islands (26 30N 128 0E) Archipelago between Kyushu and Taiwan. Some of the islands are volcanic. Sweet potatoes, sugar cane. The chief island is Okinawa, and Naha the chief town.

Sapporo Hokkaido (43 1N 141 15E) Capital of SAPPORO PREFECTURE. Pop. 1,621,000. Flour milling, brewing, sawmills. Agricultural machinery.

Sendai Honshu (38 15N 141 0E) Capital of MIYAGI PREFECTURE. Pop. 884,000. Food processing. Manufacture of metal goods, textiles, pottery. Tohoku University (1907).

Shikoku Island (33 30N 133 30E) Pop. 4,500,000. Smallest of the four main islands. Mountainous and thickly forested. Rice, tobacco, soya beans in lowlands.

Shizuoka Honshu (34 59N 138 24E) Capital of SHIZUOKA PREFECTURE. Pop. 473,000. Processing and packing of tea grown in the locality; oranges. Manufacture of machinery, chemicals.

Tokyo Honshu (35 48N 139 45E) Capital of Japan. Pop. 8.3 million. One of world's most populated cities. Shipbuilding, engineering, printing, publishing, textiles, chemicals, cars. Founded as Edo, or Yedo, in the late 12th century. Capital since 1868. Shiba Park and Ueno Park. Earthquake and fire, 1923. Severely damaged in World War II.

Toyama Honshu (36 42N 137 14E) Capital of TOYAMA PREFECTURE. Pop. 319,000. Medicines, drugs, chemicals, textiles, machinery.

Wakayama Honshu (34 10N 135 12E) Capital of WAKAYAMA PREFECTURE. Pop. 399,000. Iron, steel, textiles, chemicals, *sake.*

Yokohama Honshu (35 25N 139 35E) Capital of KANAGAWA PREFECTURE. Pop. 3.1 million. Japan's second largest city, part of conurbation. Seaport handles about one-third of Japan's foreign trade. Exports silk, synthetic fiber, canned fish. Manufactures steel, motor vehicles, chemicals. Shipbuilding, oil refinery. First Japanese port open to foreign trade (1859). Earthquake, 1923. Severely damaged in World War II.

Yokosuka (35 18N 139 39E) Pop. 431,000. Seaport and naval base on SW coast of Tokyo Bay. Shipbuilding.

Further reading

Behr, Edward. *Hirohito: The Man Behind the Myth.* New York: Random House, 1989.

Collingwood, Dean. *Japan and the Pacific Rim.* New York: Dushkin Publishers, 1990.

Dolan, Edward. *The New Japan.* New York: Franklin Watts, 1983.

Dore, Ronald P. *Shinohata: Portrait of a Japanese Village.* New York: Pantheon, 1980.

Fewster, Stuart and Gorton, Tony. *Japan from Shogun to Superstate.* New York: St. Martin's, 1988.

Greene, Carol. *Japan.* Chicago: Childrens Press, 1983.

Katzenstein, Gary. *Funny Business: An Outsider's Year in Japan.* New York: Soho Press, 1989.

Kornhauser, D. H. *Japan.* New York: Wiley & Sons, 1982.

MacDonald, Donald. *A Geography of Modern Japan.* New York: Norbury Publications, 1987.

Manning, Paul. *Hirohito: The War Years.* New York: Dodd, Mead, 1986.

Masters, Robert V. *Japan in Pictures.* Minneapolis: Lerner Publications, 1989.

Meyer, Carolyn. *A Voice from Japan: An Outsider Looks In.* New York: Harcourt, Brace, Jovanovich, 1988.

Packard, Jerrold. *Sons of Heaven: A Portrait of the Japanese Monarchy.* New York: Penguin, 1984.

Pilbeam, Morris. *Japan.* New York: Franklin Watts, 1988.

Pitts, Forrest Ralph. *Japan in the Global Community.* Grand Rapids, Mich.: Fideler Co., 1988.

Reischauer, Edwin O. *The Japanese.* Cambridge: Harvard University Press, 1977.

Sato, Hiroaki, trans. *Ten Japanese Poets.* San Francisco: Bluefish Press, 1974.

Severns, Karen. *Hirohito.* New York: Chelsea House, 1988.

Statler, Oliver. *All Japan: The Catalogue of Everything Japanese.* New York: Morrow, 1984.

Stefoff, Rebecca. *Japan.* New York: Chelsea House, 1988.

Stewart-Smith, Jo. *In the Shadow of Fujisan: Japan and Its Wildlife.* New York: Viking Penguin, 1988.

Storry, Richard. *A History of Modern Japan.* New York: Penguin, 1984.

Tames, Richard. *Passport to Japan.* New York: Franklin Watts, 1988.

Tasker, Peter. *The Japanese.* New York: Dutton, 1988.

Terry, John R. *Japan: Land of Myths.* New York: Dawn Press, 1988.

Thurley, Elizabeth E. *Through the Year in Japan.* London, UK: Batsford/Trafalgar Square Press, 1985.

Time-Life Books, Editors of. *Japan* (Library of Nations series). Alexandria, Va.: Time-Life Books, 1985.

JAPAN. Political

U.S.S.R.

Sea of Okhotsk

Occupied by the U.S.S.R since 1945
claimed by Japan pending peace treaty

U.S.S.R.

Kuril Islands

Nemuro

HOKKAIDO

Wakkanai
Haboro
Nayoro
Mombetsu
Rumoi
Takikawa
Kitami
Bihoro
Abashiri
Asahikawa
Ashibetsu
Otaru
Bibai
Furano
Iwanai
Ebetsu
Yubari
Sapporo
Chitose
Obihiro
Kushiro
Noboribetsu
Tomakomai
Yakumo
Muroran
Urakawa
Kamiiso
Hakodate

AOMORI Ohata

East from Greenwich

on same scale
as main map

SEA OF JAPAN

Sakai-minato
Izumo
Oda
TOTTORI
Yonago
Kurayoshi
Tottori
Toyooka
Tsuruga
Obama
SHIMANE
Tsuyama
Fukuchiyama
Maizuru
Nagahama
Hamada
Miyoshi
OKAYAMA
Nishiwaki
HYOGO
Ayabe
KYOTO
Otsu
Masuda
Hiroshima
Okayama
Bizen
Himeji
Toyonaka
Kakogawa
Kobe
HIROSHIMA
Kurashiki
Fukuyama
Akashi
Osaka
Hagi
Fukuyama
Mihara
Onomichi
Sakai
Higashiosaka
YAMAGUCHI
Iwakuni
KAGAWA
Kishiwada
Yamaguchi
Kure
Sumoto
NARA
seki
Hofu
Tokuyama
Sakaide
MIE
Onoda
Hikari
Takamatsu
Wakayama
Kitakyushu
Ube
Niihama
Tokushima
FUKUOKA
Matsuyama
Kawanoe
Anan
ta
EHIME
Gobo
Tanabe
izuka
OITA
KOCHI
Kochi
Shingu
Beppu
Oita
Uwajima
Muroto
Usuki
WAKAYAMA
UMAMOTO
Saiki
PACIFIC OCEAN
Kumamoto
Nobeoka
Nakamura
Hyuga
itoyoshi
MIYAZAKI

SEA OF JAPAN (north section)

Wajima
ISHIKAWA
Nanao
Himi
Takaoka
Itoigawa
Kanazawa
Toyama
Takada
NIIGATA
Komatsu
TOYAMA
Uozu
Nagano
Kaga
Naoetsu
Tokomachi
Fukui
Takayama
FUKUI
Okaya
Matsue
Takefu
GIFU
Suwa
Ueda
Saku
Njigata
Shibata
Ryotsu
Nagaoka
Aizu-wakamatsu
Murakami
Yamagata
YAMAGATA
Yonezawa
Tsuruoka
Shinjo
FUKUSHIMA
Sakata
Shiroishi
MIYAGI
Shiogama
Soma
Fukushima
Koriyama
Iwaki
Shiroishi
Sendai
Ishinomaki
AKITA
Akita
Yokote
IWATE
Kamaishi
Noshiro
Oga
Odate
Morioka
Ichinoseki
Ofunato
Kesennuma
HOKKAIDO
Aomori
Hirosaki
Misawa
AOMORI
Towada
Hachinohe
Ohata

Central honshu
Seki
Iida
Ina
GIFU
Tajami
Gifu
Ogaki
Seto
Nagoya
Kasugai
Ichinomiya
AICHI
Kozaki
Yokkaichi
Toyokawa
Handa
Suzaka
Toyohashi
Tsu
Matsuzaka
Ise
Toba
Kumano
Owase

Tokyo region
GUMMA
Numata
Kanuma
Kiryu
TOCHIGI
Takasaki
Utsunomiya
Kumagaya
Oyama
Mito
SAITAMA
IBARAKI
Omiya
Tsuchiura
Ashikaga
Nakaminato
Kawagoe
Urawa
Kashiwa
Hitachi
Kofu
Fuji-yoshida
YAMANASHI
TOKYO
Funabashi
Chiba
Fujinomiya
Shimizu
TOKYO
Yokohama
Choshi
Kawasaki
Fuji
Numazu
Atami
CHIBA
Shizuoka
Yaizu
Yokosuka
Mobara
SHIZUOKA
Hiratsuka
Iwata
Shimada
Tateyama
Hamamatsu

S. KOREA

Masan
PUSAN
S. KOREA
Sea of Japan
SHIMANE
Hamada
Masuda
Hiroshim
YAMAGUCHI
Hagi
Yamaguchi
Hofu
Izuhara
Shimonoseki
Onoda
Tokuyam
Kitakyushu
Ube
Hikari
FUKUOKA
Karatsu
Iizuka
Usa
Yawataha
Fukuoka
Hirado
SAGA
Imari
Hita
OITA
EHIM
Sasebo
Omura
Saga
Kurume
Beppu
Oita
NAGASAKI
Omuta
Usuki
Hondo
KUMAMOTO
Nagasaki
Shimabara
Kumamoto
Saiki
Minamata
Yatsushiro
MIYAZAKI
Nobeoka
Hyuga
Hitoyoshi
Sendai
Miyakonojo
Kagoshima
Nichinan
Kanoya
KAGOSHIMA

on same scale as main map

East from Greenwich

Shanghai
Ningpo
RYUKYU ISLANDS
continuation southwards
Miyazaki
Kagoshima
East
China
Sea
Naze
TAIPEI
TAIWAN
Naha
Koza
PACIFIC OCEAN
East
China Sea

Scale 1:15,000,000

0   100 miles
0   100 kilometres

Legend

International Boundaries	Railways

Cities and Towns	Motorways

Prefecture Boundaries	Main airports

Prefectures numbered on map

1   KANAGAWA
2   OSAKA

Canals

Scale 1:5,000,000

0   25   50   75   100 miles
0   25   50   75   100 kilometres

Projection: Conical

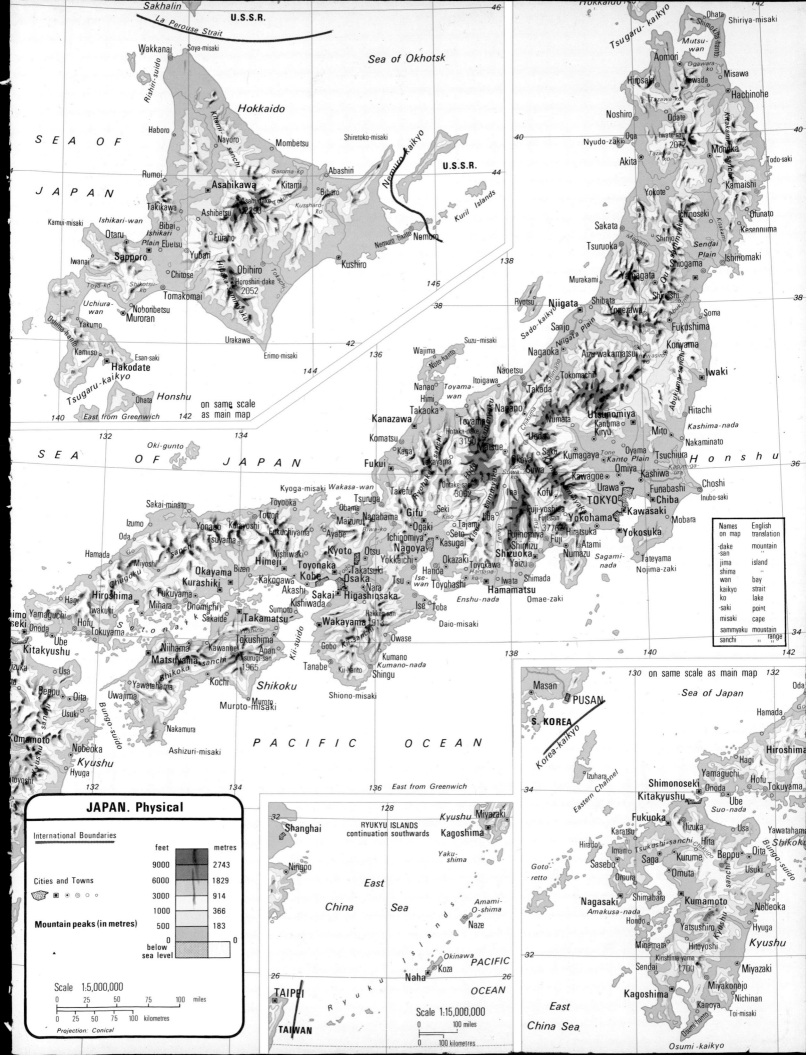

JAPAN. Physical

Index